I0479094

2023

RETIREMENT

PLANNING GUIDE

How to Design a Fulfilling Life in Your Senior Years

Larry Reeves

TABLE OF CONTENTS

Introduction 6
I. Retirement Planning 6
II. What to Expect from this Guide 9
III. How to Use this Guide 12

Chapter 1: Understanding Retirement Planning 15
I. Definition of Retirement Planning 15
II. Why Planning is Crucial 17
III. Common Mistakes to Avoid 20
IV. Retirement Planning Checklist 26

Chapter 2: Assessing Your Retirement Needs 31
I. Estimating Retirement Expenses 31
II. Evaluating Retirement Income sources 34
III. How to Calculate Retirement Savings Goal 38
IV. Adjusting Retirement Plan for Inflation 42

Chapter 3: Developing Your Retirement Plan 48
1. Types of Retirement Plans 48
II. Key Components of a Retirement Plan 53
III. How to Create a Retirement Budget 57

IV. Retirement Savings Goal Strategies   60

Chapter 4: Investing for Retirement   63
I. Investment Strategies   63
II. Understanding Retirement Accounts   66
III. Choosing Right Investments Portfolio   70
IV. Investment Options: Risk/Benefits   75

Chapter 5: Maximizing Social Security Benefits 80
I. Understanding Social Security Benefits   80
II. Maximize Your Social Security Benefits   82
III. Factors Affecting Social Security Benefits 86
IV. When to Claim Social Security Benefits   89

Chapter 6: Managing Retirement Income   93
I. Retirement Income Strategies   93
II. Sustainable Retirement Income Plan   97
III. Different Income Sources Tax Implication 100
IV. Strategies for Managing Income   104

Chapter 7: Estate Planning In Retirement   108
I. Importance of Estate Planning   108
II. Key Elements of Estate Plannin   111
III. Creating Comprehensive Estate Plan   115
IV. Estate Planning Mistakes to Avoid   116

CHAPTER 8: Conclusion   121

I. Recap of Key Points   121

II. Retirement Planning Journey: Next Sreps 124

III. Resources for Further Learning   126

Acknowledgements   130

INTRODUCTION

I. **Retirement Planning & it's Importance**

Retirement is a significant milestone in our lives, marking the end of our working years and the beginning of a new chapter. As we enter our senior years, retirement planning becomes an essential aspect of our financial well-being.

Retirement planning is the process of identifying your retirement income goals, estimating your future expenses, and creating a plan to achieve your financial objectives. It is crucial to start planning for retirement early to ensure you have enough funds to support your lifestyle and expenses during your golden years.

Retirement planning is crucial for several reasons. Firstly, it allows you to maintain your standard of living even after you retire. Without a plan in place, you may not have enough money to cover your living expenses, healthcare costs, and other essential needs. Retirement planning helps you calculate how much you need to save to maintain your current lifestyle during your retirement years.

Secondly, retirement planning gives you peace of mind. Knowing that you have enough funds to cover your expenses during your retirement years can alleviate stress and anxiety about your future financial situation. It allows you to focus on enjoying your retirement and pursuing your passions without worrying about money.

Thirdly, retirement planning allows you to take advantage of tax-efficient strategies to maximize your retirement income. By planning ahead, you can identify tax-efficient investment vehicles and create a withdrawal strategy that minimizes your tax burden while maximizing your retirement income.

Finally, retirement planning is essential for leaving a legacy. A well-planned retirement can provide for your loved ones and ensure that your assets are distributed according to your wishes. Estate planning is an integral part of retirement planning and can help you protect your assets and provide for your family's future.

In conclusion, retirement planning is crucial for achieving financial security and a fulfilling life during your golden years. It is never too early or too late to start planning for retirement, and the benefits of a well-planned retirement are numerous.

II. What to Expect from this Guide

This retirement planning guide aims to provide you with a comprehensive understanding of retirement planning and help you design a fulfilling life during your senior years. The guide is designed to take you through the various stages of retirement planning, from understanding its importance to estate planning.

In this guide, you can expect to learn about the following:

- The importance of retirement planning and the consequences of not planning
- How to assess your retirement needs and calculate your retirement savings goal
- Different types of retirement plans and how to create a retirement budget
- Investment strategies for retirement and how to choose the right investments for your portfolio

- Maximizing your social security benefits and creating a sustainable retirement income plan
- The importance of estate planning and how to create a comprehensive estate plan

Throughout the guide, you will find practical tips and advice to help you make informed decisions about your retirement planning. You will also find resources and tools to help you create a retirement plan that meets your unique needs and goals.

By the end of this guide, you will have a solid understanding of retirement planning and the tools and knowledge necessary to create a fulfilling life during your senior years.

III. **How to Use this Guide**:

This retirement planning guide is designed to be user-friendly and easy to navigate. To get the most out of this guide, I recommend following these steps:

Step 1: Read the Introduction: Start by reading the introduction to understand the importance of retirement planning and what to expect from this guide.

Step 2: Read Each Chapter: Each chapter is designed to cover a specific aspect of retirement planning. It's recommended reading each chapter in order to ensure a comprehensive understanding of retirement planning.

Step 3: Complete the Checklists: Reading the guide, you will find checklists that will help you assess your retirement needs, create a retirement budget, and evaluate your retirement income sources. It's recommended that you complete these checklists as you read the corresponding chapters.

Step 4: Use the Resources: The guide provides resources and tools to help you with retirement planning. I recommend using these resources to supplement your learning and ensure you have everything you need to plan for a fulfilling retirement.

Step 5: Take Action: Retirement planning requires action. Once you have read the guide and completed the checklists, it's time to take action. Use the knowledge you have gained to create a retirement plan that meets your unique needs and goals.

By following these steps, you can use this guide to create a comprehensive retirement plan and design a fulfilling life in your senior years.

CHAPTER 1

UNDERSTANDING RETIREMENT PLANNING

I. Definition of Retirement Planning

Retirement planning is the process of identifying your retirement income goals, estimating your future expenses, and creating a plan to achieve your financial objectives. It involves evaluating your current financial situation, projecting your retirement income needs, and creating a strategy to save and invest your money to achieve your retirement goals.

Retirement planning is essential to ensure that you have enough funds to support your lifestyle and expenses during your retirement years. It is a proactive approach to financial management that helps you create a sustainable income stream that can last for the rest of your life.

Retirement planning requires a long-term perspective and a comprehensive approach to your finances. It involves evaluating your income sources, creating a budget, and identifying ways to maximize your retirement income. It also includes assessing your risk tolerance, choosing the right investment vehicles, and creating an estate plan.

In short, retirement planning is a critical aspect of financial planning that helps you achieve financial security and a fulfilling life during your senior years. It is never too early or too late to start retirement planning, and the benefits of a well-planned retirement are numerous.

II. Why Retirement Planning is Crucial

Retirement planning is crucial for several reasons, including the following:

1. **Ensuring Financial Security:** Retirement planning helps ensure that you have enough funds to maintain your lifestyle and cover your expenses during your retirement years. Without a

proper retirement plan, you may be at risk of running out of money in your senior years.

2. Maximizing Retirement Income: Retirement planning helps you maximize your retirement income by identifying the best income sources, creating a budget, and investing your money wisely. A well-planned retirement can provide a comfortable income stream that lasts throughout your life.

3. Managing Retirement Risks: Retirement planning helps you manage various risks associated with retirement, such as inflation, market volatility, and longevity risk. By creating a diversified investment portfolio and choosing the right insurance products, you can mitigate these risks and protect your retirement savings.

4. Creating a Fulfilling Retirement: Retirement planning helps you design a fulfilling retirement by identifying your retirement goals and creating a plan to achieve them. A well-planned retirement can provide you with the financial security and freedom to pursue your interests, hobbies, and travel goals.

In summary, retirement planning is crucial for ensuring financial security, maximizing retirement income, managing retirement risks, and creating a fulfilling retirement. It is an essential aspect of financial planning that requires a long-term perspective and a comprehensive approach to your finances.

III. Common Retirement Planning Mistakes to Avoid

Retirement planning is a complex process that requires careful consideration of various factors, such as income sources, expenses, investment strategies, and risk tolerance. Despite the importance of retirement planning, many individuals make common mistakes that can undermine their retirement goals.

Here are some of the most common retirement planning mistakes to avoid:

1. Underestimating Retirement Expenses

Many individuals underestimate their retirement expenses and assume that their expenses will decrease during retirement. However, in reality, many expenses, such as healthcare costs and travel expenses, may increase during retirement. To avoid this mistake, it is essential to create a realistic budget that accounts for all potential expenses during retirement.

2. Starting Retirement Planning Too Late

Many individuals delay retirement planning until later in life, which can make it challenging to achieve their retirement goals. Starting early and creating a comprehensive retirement plan can provide more time to save, invest, and adjust the plan as needed.

3. Failing to Diversify Investments

Many individuals make the mistake of putting all their retirement savings into one investment, such as company stock or real estate. However, this can expose them to unnecessary risk and volatility. Diversifying investments across different asset classes, such as stocks, bonds, and real estate, can help manage risk and maximize returns.

4. Ignoring Tax Implications

Taxes can have a significant impact on retirement savings and income. Failing to account for tax implications, such as taxes on retirement account withdrawals and Social Security benefits, can result in lower retirement income. To avoid this mistake, it is essential to understand the tax implications of retirement savings and income and plan accordingly.

5. Overlooking Longevity Risk

Many individuals underestimate their life expectancy and assume they will not live as long as they do. This can lead to running out of money during retirement. To avoid this mistake, it is essential to plan for a longer life expectancy and create a retirement plan that accounts for potential longevity risk.

6. Failing to Revisit and Adjust Retirement Plan

Life circumstances can change, and retirement plans may need to be adjusted accordingly. Failing to revisit and adjust the retirement plan regularly can result in an outdated plan that no longer meets retirement goals. To avoid this mistake, it is essential to review and adjust the retirement plan regularly as needed.

7. Not Maximizing Retirement Contributions

Many individuals do not maximize their retirement contributions, such as 401(k) contributions or IRA contributions. Failing to maximize retirement contributions can result in lower retirement savings and income. To avoid this mistake, it is essential to contribute as much as possible to retirement accounts each year.

8. Relying Too Much on Social Security

Social Security benefits are a crucial part of retirement income for many individuals, but they may not be enough to cover all retirement expenses. Relying too much on Social Security can result in a lower standard of living during retirement. To avoid this mistake, it is essential to create a retirement plan that accounts for all potential sources of retirement income.

Examples of these common retirement planning mistakes can include:

- Underestimating healthcare costs during retirement and not accounting for it in the budget
- Waiting too long to start saving for retirement and missing out on years of compound interest
- Investing all retirement savings in one company stock, which can result in significant losses if the company performs poorly
- Withdrawing too much money from a retirement account and not
- accounting for taxes, resulting in a lower retirement income
- Assuming a shorter life expectancy and not planning for potential medical expenses and

living costs during a longer retirement

- Failing to adjust retirement plans after a significant life event, such as a divorce or job loss
- Contributing only the minimum amount to retirement accounts and missing out on potential tax benefits and employer contributions.

IV. Retirement Planning Checklist

Retirement planning can be a complex process, but having a checklist can help ensure that all important steps are taken to prepare for retirement.

Here is a retirement planning checklist to help guide individuals through the retirement planning process:

1. Determine retirement goals and desired lifestyle

Before creating a retirement plan, it is essential to determine what retirement goals and lifestyle the individual wants to achieve. This can help guide decisions related to income, expenses, and investment strategies.

2. Estimate retirement expenses

It is important to estimate expected retirement expenses, including both essential and discretionary expenses. This can help create a realistic budget and determine how much retirement income is needed.

3. Assess current retirement savings

Review all retirement savings accounts, such as 401(k) or IRA accounts, and determine the current balance and contribution rate.

4. Calculate retirement income: Estimate all potential sources of retirement income, such as Social Security benefits, pension benefits, and investment income.

5. Determine retirement age

Determine the desired retirement age and the age at which Social Security benefits will be received.

6. Create a retirement plan

Based on retirement goals, expected expenses, and retirement income, create a comprehensive retirement plan that includes strategies for saving, investing, and managing retirement income.

7. Revisit and adjust the retirement plan

Review the retirement plan regularly, at least once per year, and adjust the plan as needed based on changes in circumstances or goals.

8. Maximize retirement contributions

Contribute as much as possible to retirement accounts each year, taking advantage of any employer contributions or tax benefits.

9. Diversify investments

Diversify retirement investments across different asset classes, such as stocks, bonds, and real estate, to manage risk and maximize returns.

10: Plan for healthcare costs

Estimate potential healthcare costs during retirement and plan for them accordingly, including purchasing supplemental health insurance or long-term care insurance if necessary.

11. Consider tax implications

Understand the tax implications of retirement savings and income and plan accordingly, such as taking advantage of tax-advantaged retirement accounts.

12: Plan for longevity risk

Plan for a longer life expectancy and create a retirement plan that accounts for potential longevity risk, including inflation and increased healthcare costs.

By following this retirement planning checklist, individuals can help ensure that they are taking all necessary steps to prepare for a fulfilling retirement.

CHAPTER 2:

ASSESSING YOUR RETIREMENT NEEDS

I. Estimating Your Retirement Expenses

One of the key steps in retirement planning is estimating the amount of money you will need to cover your expenses during retirement. To estimate your retirement expenses, consider the following factors:

1. **Housing expenses:** This includes mortgage or rent payments, property taxes, and homeowners or renters insurance.

2. **Food and groceries:** Estimate your monthly food expenses based on your current spending habits.
3. **Transportation:** Estimate your transportation costs, including car payments, gas, maintenance, and insurance.
4. **Healthcare:** Estimate your potential healthcare expenses, including insurance premiums, deductibles, and copays.
5. **Leisure activities:** Estimate the cost of leisure activities, such as travel, hobbies, and entertainment.
6. **Utilities:** Estimate your monthly utility expenses, including electricity, gas, water, and phone and internet bills.
7. **Debts:** Include any outstanding debts, such as credit card debt or

student loans, that you will need to pay during retirement.

8. **Miscellaneous expenses:** This includes expenses such as clothing, personal care, and gifts.

When estimating your retirement expenses, it is important to consider both essential and discretionary expenses. Essential expenses are necessary for day-to-day living, while discretionary expenses are non-essential and can be reduced or eliminated if necessary.

Once you have estimated your retirement expenses, you can compare this amount to your expected

retirement income to determine if you have enough saved for retirement. If your estimated expenses exceed your expected income, you may need to adjust your retirement plan to increase your savings or reduce your expenses.

It is important to remember that estimating retirement expenses is not an exact science and unexpected expenses can arise during retirement. Regularly reviewing and adjusting your retirement plan can help ensure that you are adequately prepared for retirement.

II. Evaluating Your Sources of Retirement Income

In addition to estimating your retirement expenses, it is important to evaluate your sources of retirement income. Consider the following potential sources of retirement income:

1. **Social Security:** This is a government program that provides retirement income to eligible individuals. The amount of Social Security benefits you will receive depends on your work history and the age at which you begin receiving benefits.

2. **Pension plans:** Some employers offer pension plans that provide retirement income to eligible employees. The amount of pension benefits you will receive depends on factors such as your years of service and salary history.

3. **Personal savings:** This includes any savings and investment accounts that you have accumulated during your working years, such as individual retirement accounts (IRAs) or 401(k) plans.

4. **Rental income:** If you own rental property, this can provide additional retirement income.
5. **Annuities:** An annuity is a financial product that provides a guaranteed stream of income during retirement in exchange for an upfront payment.
6. **Part-time work:** Some retirees choose to work part-time to supplement their retirement income.

When evaluating your sources of retirement income, it is important to consider the reliability and sustainability of each source. For example, Social Security benefits are guaranteed by the government, while the sustainability of personal savings and investment income can vary depending on market conditions.

It is also important to consider the tax implications of each source of retirement income. For example, Social Security benefits may be taxable, while withdrawals from traditional IRAs and 401(k) plans are generally taxed as ordinary income.

By evaluating your sources of retirement income, you can better understand your retirement income streams and determine if you have enough income to cover your estimated retirement expenses. If your expected retirement income falls short of your estimated expenses, you may need to adjust your retirement plan to increase your savings or reduce your expenses.

III. How to Calculate Your Retirement Savings Goal

One of the most important steps in retirement planning is determining how much money you will need to save to achieve your retirement goals. Calculating your retirement savings goal can be a complex process, but there are some basic steps you can follow to estimate the amount you will need to save.

Step 1: Estimate Your Retirement Expenses

As discussed earlier, the first step in calculating your retirement savings goal is to estimate your retirement expenses. This includes essential expenses such as housing, food, and healthcare, as well as discretionary expenses such as travel and hobbies.

Step 2: Determine Your Retirement Income Needs

Next, you will need to determine how much income you will need during retirement to cover your estimated expenses. This includes income from sources such as Social Security, pensions, and personal savings.

Step 3: Determine Your Retirement Age and Life Expectancy

The age at which you plan to retire and your life expectancy are important factors in calculating your retirement savings goal. The earlier you retire and the longer you live, the more money you will need to save to support your retirement lifestyle.

Step 4: Calculate Your Retirement Savings Goal

Once you have estimated your retirement expenses, determined your retirement income needs, and established your retirement age and life expectancy, you can calculate your retirement savings goal. A common method is to use the "4% rule," which suggests that you can safely withdraw 4% of your retirement savings each year to cover your retirement expenses without running out of money.

For example, if you estimate that you will need $50,000 per year in retirement income and you expect to receive $25,000 per year from Social Security and pensions, you will need to generate an additional $25,000 per year in retirement income from your personal savings. Using the 4% rule, you can calculate that you will need to save $625,000 ($25,000 ÷ 0.04) to generate this income.

It is important to remember that these calculations are just estimates and there are many factors that can impact your retirement savings needs, such as inflation, market conditions, and unexpected expenses. Regularly reviewing and adjusting your retirement plan can help ensure that you are on track to achieve your retirement goals.

In addition to the above steps, there are several retirement savings calculators available online that can help you estimate your retirement savings goal based on your individual circumstances. These calculators take into account factors such as your current age, retirement age, expected

Social Security benefits, and current savings to provide an estimate of the amount you will need to save to achieve your retirement goals.

In conclusion, calculating your retirement savings goal is an important step in retirement planning. By estimating your retirement expenses, determining your retirement income needs, and taking into account your retirement age and life expectancy, you can establish a realistic savings goal and develop a retirement plan that can help you achieve your goals.

IV. Adjusting Your Retirement Plan for Inflation

Inflation is the increase in the prices of goods and services over time. It affects the purchasing power of your money and can have a significant impact on your retirement plan.

When you retire, you will need to have enough money to cover your expenses throughout your retirement, which could last for decades. This means you will need to plan for inflation and adjust your retirement plan accordingly.

Here are some steps you can take to adjust your retirement plan for inflation:

Step 1: Understand the Impact of Inflation on Your Retirement Plan

The first step in adjusting your retirement plan for inflation is to understand how inflation can impact your plan. Inflation can erode the purchasing power of your savings, meaning that the money you saved may not be worth as much in the future. This can make it difficult to maintain your desired lifestyle in retirement, especially if you have a fixed income.

Step 2: Consider Inflation-Adjusted Retirement Income Sources

To mitigate the impact of inflation on your retirement income, consider sources of income that are adjusted for inflation. Social Security benefits, for

example, are adjusted annually for inflation. Annuities and other types of investments that provide inflation-adjusted income can also be a good option.

Step 3: Use a Realistic Inflation Rate in Your Retirement Plan

When creating your retirement plan, it is important to use a realistic inflation rate. The historical average inflation rate in the United States is around 3%, but inflation rates can vary widely from year to year. Consider using a conservative estimate to ensure that you are prepared for the impact of inflation on your savings.

Step 4: Plan for Increased Expenses in Retirement

In addition to adjusting your income for inflation, it is important to plan for increased expenses in retirement. Healthcare costs, for example, tend to increase faster than the overall inflation rate. Long-term care expenses and travel costs can also increase significantly over time. By factoring in these potential increased expenses, you can ensure that your retirement plan is prepared for the impact of inflation.

Step 5: Regularly Review and Adjust Your Retirement Plan

Finally, it is important to regularly review and adjust your retirement plan to account for changes in your expenses, income, and inflation rate. By regularly monitoring your retirement plan, you can ensure that you are on track to meet your retirement goals and adjust your plan as necessary to account for changes in your financial situation.

In conclusion, adjusting your retirement plan for inflation is an important step in retirement planning. By understanding the impact of inflation on your savings, considering inflation-adjusted income sources, using a realistic inflation rate, planning for increased expenses, and regularly reviewing and adjusting your plan, you can help ensure that you are prepared for the impact of inflation on your retirement.

CHAPTER 3

DEVELOPING YOUR RETIREMENT PLAN

1. Types of Retirement Plans

When it comes to developing a retirement plan, one of the first things you need to consider is the type of retirement plan that will work best for you. There are several types of retirement plans available, each with its own benefits and drawbacks. In this chapter, we'll take a closer look at the most common types of retirement plans.

401(k) Plans

A 401(k) plan is a type of employer-sponsored retirement plan that allows employees to save for retirement on a pre-tax basis. Contributions are deducted directly from your paycheck, and the funds in the plan grow tax-free until you withdraw them in retirement. Many employers also offer a matching contribution, which can help you save even more.

Traditional IRA

A traditional IRA is an individual retirement account that allows you to make tax-deductible contributions up to a certain amount each year. The funds in the account grow tax-free until you withdraw them in retirement.

However, when you withdraw the funds, you'll pay income tax on them.

Roth IRA

A Roth IRA is another type of individual retirement account, but with a different tax structure. With a Roth IRA, you make contributions with after-tax dollars, meaning you've already paid taxes on the money. The funds in the account then grow tax-free, and when you withdraw them in retirement, you won't have to pay any taxes on them.

Simplified Employee Pension (SEP) Plan

A SEP plan is a retirement plan for small businesses and self-employed individuals. With a SEP plan, the employer makes contributions on behalf of the employees, and the contributions are tax-deductible for the employer. The funds in the plan grow tax-free until the employee withdraws them in retirement.

Defined Benefit Plan

A defined benefit plan is a traditional pension plan that guarantees a specific benefit amount to the employee upon retirement. The benefit amount is typically based on the employee's salary and years of service. The employer is responsible for funding the plan, and the employee receives a set amount each month in retirement.

Cash Balance Plan

A cash balance plan is a type of defined benefit plan that's becoming increasingly popular. With a cash balance plan, the employer contributes a set amount each year on behalf of the employee, and the funds in the plan grow tax-free until the employee withdraws them in retirement. When the employee retires, they can choose to take the balance as a lump sum or receive monthly payments.

Non-Qualified Deferred Compensation Plan

A non-qualified deferred compensation plan is a type of retirement plan that's typically offered to high-level executives. With this type of plan, employees defer a portion of their income to the plan, and the funds grow tax-free until the employee withdraws them in retirement. Unlike other retirement plans, there are no contribution limits with a non-qualified deferred compensation plan.

Overall, choosing the right retirement plan is crucial to achieving your retirement goals. Each type of retirement plan has its own benefits and drawbacks, so it's important to do your research and speak with a financial advisor to determine which plan is best for you based on your individual circumstances.

II. Key Components of a Retirement Plan

When it comes to developing a retirement plan, there are several key components that are essential to consider. These components can help ensure that you have a solid plan in place that meets your financial needs and goals during retirement.

In this section, we will discuss some of the most important components of a retirement plan.

Retirement goals and objectives: The first component of a retirement plan is to establish clear goals and objectives. This includes determining when you want to retire, how much income you will need in retirement, and what lifestyle you want to maintain. Having a clear idea of your retirement goals and objectives will help you make informed decisions about your retirement savings and investment strategies.

Retirement income sources: The next component of a retirement plan is to identify your sources of retirement income. This can include Social Security, pensions, retirement accounts, and other sources of income. It is important to understand the amount and timing of each source of income to create a comprehensive retirement plan.

Savings and investment strategies: Another important component of a retirement plan is to establish savings and investment strategies that align with your retirement goals and objectives. This may include investing in retirement accounts such as 401(k) plans or IRAs, as well as other investment options such as stocks, bonds, and real estate. It is important to balance risk and return based on your individual needs and goals.

Risk management: As you develop your retirement plan, it is important to consider the potential risks that could impact your retirement income and savings. This includes market volatility, inflation, and longevity risk. You may want to consider strategies such as diversification, asset allocation, and insurance to manage these risks.

Estate planning: The final component of a retirement plan is estate planning. This involves creating a plan for the distribution of your assets after you pass away. This can include creating a will, establishing a trust, and planning for any tax implications.

In summary, a retirement plan should include clear goals and objectives, an understanding of retirement income sources, savings and investment strategies, risk management, and estate planning. By considering these key components, you can create a comprehensive retirement plan that meets your individual needs and goals.

III. How to Create a Retirement Budget

Creating a retirement budget is an essential step in developing a retirement plan. A retirement budget helps you estimate your expected expenses and determine how much money you need to save for retirement.

Here are the steps to create a retirement budget:

1. **Estimate your expenses:** The first step is to estimate your expenses in retirement. This includes basic living expenses such as housing, food, utilities, transportation, and healthcare. You should also include discretionary expenses

such as travel, hobbies, and entertainment.

2. **Consider inflation**: Inflation can significantly impact your retirement expenses. It's essential to factor in inflation when estimating your expenses. Generally, inflation averages around 3% annually.

3. **Calculate your retirement income**: Your retirement income includes any sources of income such as Social Security, pension, and retirement savings. You should calculate your retirement income based on your estimated retirement age and the age you plan to begin receiving Social Security benefits.

4. **Determine any gaps in your retirement income**: Once you have estimated your expenses and

retirement income, you can determine if there are any gaps. If your retirement income is less than your estimated expenses, you will need to save more to fill the gap.

5. **Adjust your expenses:** If you have a gap between your retirement income and expenses, you may need to adjust your expenses. This may include downsizing your home, reducing discretionary spending, or delaying retirement.

6. **Monitor and adjust your retirement budget:** Your retirement budget is not set in stone. You should monitor your expenses and income regularly and adjust your budget as needed.

Creating a retirement budget can seem overwhelming, but it's an essential step in planning for retirement. It helps you understand your expected expenses and income, and identify any gaps that need to be filled.

With a well-planned retirement budget, you can feel confident that you are on track to achieve your retirement goals.

IV. Strategies for Achieving Your Retirement Savings Goal

There are several strategies you can employ to help you achieve your retirement savings goal.

Here are a few:

1. **Start saving early:** The earlier you start saving for retirement, the more time your money has to

grow. Even if you can only save a small amount each month, it can add up over time.

2. **Maximize contributions to retirement accounts:** Contribute as much as you can to your 401(k), IRA, or other retirement accounts. If your employer offers a match, make sure you contribute enough to take advantage of it.

3. **Use a retirement calculator:** Use a retirement calculator to help you determine how much you need to save to achieve your retirement savings goal. This can help you create a realistic plan for saving and investing.

4. **Adjust your expenses:** Look for ways to reduce your expenses so you can save more for retirement. This may involve cutting back on discretionary spending or finding

ways to reduce fixed expenses like housing costs.

5. **Invest wisely:** Choose investments that are appropriate for your risk tolerance and investment goals. Diversify your portfolio to minimize risk and maximize returns.

6. **Consider working longer:** If you're behind on your retirement savings, you may need to work longer to save more. Working even a few extra years can significantly boost your retirement savings.

7. **Seek professional advice:** Consider working with a financial advisor or planner who can help you create a customized retirement plan and provide guidance on how to achieve your retirement savings goals.

CHAPTER 4

INVESTING FOR RETIREMENT

I. Investment Strategies for Retirement

Investing for retirement requires a long-term perspective and a focus on building a diversified portfolio that can help you meet your financial goals. Here are some investment strategies that can help you achieve your retirement goals:

Asset Allocation: The first step in developing an investment strategy for retirement is to determine your asset allocation. This involves deciding how much of your portfolio you will allocate to stocks, bonds, and other asset classes. The appropriate allocation will depend on your age, risk tolerance, and investment objectives.

Diversification: Diversification is the key to reducing risk in your portfolio. By investing in a variety of asset classes, you can help protect yourself from market volatility and minimize the impact of any one investment on your overall portfolio.

Retirement Funds: Retirement funds, such as target-date funds, are designed to automatically adjust your asset allocation as you approach retirement. These funds can be a good option for investors who want a simple, low-maintenance investment strategy.

Income-Producing Investments: As you approach retirement, it's important to focus on investments that generate income. This can include dividend-paying stocks, bonds, and real estate investment trusts (REITs).

Consider Working with a Financial Advisor: A financial advisor can help you develop a retirement investment strategy that is tailored to your individual needs and goals. They can also help you stay on track with regular portfolio reviews and adjustments.

Ultimately, the key to successful retirement investing is to start early, invest regularly, and maintain a long-term perspective. By following these investment strategies, you can help ensure that you have the financial resources you need to enjoy a comfortable retirement.

II. Understanding Retirement Accounts (401(k), IRA, Roth IRA, etc.

There are several types of retirement accounts available, each with its own benefits and rules. Here is a breakdown of some of the most common retirement accounts:

1. 401(k)

A 401(k) is a tax-advantaged retirement savings plan offered by many employers. Contributions are made pre-tax, which means you don't pay taxes on the money until you withdraw it in retirement. Many employers also offer a matching contribution up to a certain percentage of your salary, which can help boost your savings.

2. Traditional IRA

A traditional IRA is an individual retirement account that allows you to make tax-deductible contributions up to a certain amount each year (as of 2021, the limit is $6,000 for those under age 50 and $7,000 for those 50 and over). The money grows tax-free until you withdraw it in retirement, at which point it is taxed as ordinary income.

3. Roth IRA

A Roth IRA is similar to a traditional IRA, but contributions are made with after-tax dollars. The money grows tax-free, and withdrawals in retirement are also tax-free. One of the advantages of a Roth IRA is that you can withdraw your contributions at any time without penalty.

4. SEP IRA

A Simplified Employee Pension (SEP) IRA is a retirement plan for self-employed individuals and small business owners. Contributions are tax-deductible and grow tax-free until retirement, at which point they are taxed as ordinary income.

5. Solo 401(k)

A Solo 401(k) is a retirement plan for self-employed individuals with no employees (other than a spouse). It allows you to contribute both as an employer and an employee, up to a certain limit each year.

6. SIMPLE IRA

A Savings Incentive Match Plan for Employees (SIMPLE) IRA is a retirement plan for small businesses with up to 100 employees. Both employers and employees can make contributions, and contributions are tax-deductible for the employer and tax-deferred for the employee.

It's important to understand the rules and limits for each type of retirement account, as they can vary depending on your age, income, and employment status. For example, there are different contribution limits for traditional and Roth IRAs based on your income and age, and some retirement plans have vesting requirements that dictate when you are eligible to withdraw funds.

Overall, retirement accounts can be a powerful tool for saving for retirement and reducing your tax burden. By understanding the different types of retirement accounts and their benefits you can make informed decisions about how to save for your future.

III. How to Choose the Right Investments for Your Retirement Portfolio

When it comes to choosing the right investments for your retirement portfolio, there are a few important factors to consider:

1. **Risk Tolerance:** The amount of risk you're willing to take on in your investments is an important factor to consider. Generally, younger investors can afford to take on more risk since they have a longer time horizon to weather market fluctuations. As you

approach retirement age, however, it may be prudent to shift toward more conservative investments to protect your savings.

2. **Diversification:** It's important to diversify your portfolio by investing in a mix of different asset classes, such as stocks, bonds, and real estate, to reduce your risk of loss. Different types of assets tend to perform differently in different market conditions, so diversification can help balance your portfolio's overall performance.

3. **Fees and Expenses:** Be aware of the fees and expenses associated with different investment options. High fees can eat into your returns over time, so look for low-cost investment options like index

funds and exchange-traded funds (ETFs).

4. **Tax Considerations:** Retirement accounts like 401(k)s and IRAs offer tax advantages that can help boost your savings over time. Be sure to understand the tax implications of your investment choices and consider working with a financial advisor or tax professional to optimize your retirement savings strategy.

5. **Your Retirement Goals:** Your investment choices should align with your retirement goals, such as when you plan to retire, your desired lifestyle, and your expected expenses in retirement. This will help you determine how much you need to save and how aggressively you should invest to reach your goals.

When choosing specific investments, there are a variety of options to consider. Some common investment choices for retirement portfolios include:

1. **Stocks:** Stocks can provide long-term growth potential, but they also come with more risk than other investment options. Consider investing in a mix of large-cap, mid-cap, and small-cap stocks to diversify your portfolio.
2. **Bonds:** Bonds are generally less risky than stocks and can provide a steady stream of income. Consider investing in a mix of government, municipal, and corporate bonds to diversify your portfolio.

3. **Real Estate:** Real estate can provide a stable source of income and may appreciate in value over time. Consider investing in real estate investment trusts (REITs) or rental properties to diversify your portfolio.

4. **Mutual Funds and ETFs:** Mutual funds and ETFs are diversified investment options that can provide exposure to a mix of stocks, bonds, and other asset classes. Look for low-cost index funds or ETFs to keep fees low.

5. **Target-Date Funds:** Target-date funds are a type of mutual fund that automatically adjust their asset allocation as you approach retirement age. These funds can be a good choice for investors who want a hands-off approach to investing for retirement.

Ultimately, the right investment choices for your retirement portfolio will depend on your individual goals, risk tolerance, and financial situation. Consider working with a financial advisor or doing your own research to make informed investment decisions that align with your retirement goals.

IV. Risks and Benefits of Different Investment Options

Investing for retirement comes with its own set of risks and benefits. It is important to understand them so that you can make informed decisions when selecting investment options for your retirement portfolio.

Here are some of the risks and benefits of different investment options:

1. Stocks

- **Risks:** Market volatility and fluctuations can cause significant losses. Individual company risks such as bankruptcy or management changes can impact stock prices.
- **Benefits:** Historically, stocks have provided high returns over the long term. Diversification across different sectors and regions can reduce individual company risks.

2. Bonds

- **Risks:** Interest rate changes can impact bond prices and yields. Credit risks associated with the issuer can impact bond prices.
- **Benefits:** Bonds generally provide stable and predictable returns.

Bonds can diversify a portfolio and provide a source of income.

3. Real Estate

- **Risks**: Real estate prices can be highly volatile. The costs of maintenance and repair can be significant.
- **Benefits**: Real estate can provide a steady stream of rental income. Real estate can serve as a hedge against inflation.

4. Mutual Funds

- **Risks**: Mutual funds are subject to market risks. Fees and expenses associated with mutual funds can reduce overall returns.
- **Benefits**: Mutual funds offer diversification across multiple stocks or bonds. Professional

management can provide expertise and guidance.

5. Exchange Traded Funds (ETFs)

- **Risks**: ETFs are subject to market risks. Some ETFs may have lower liquidity than others.
- **Benefits**: ETFs offer diversification across multiple stocks or bonds. Lower fees and expenses compared to mutual funds.

Annuities

- **Risks**: Annuities can be complex and difficult to understand. Some annuities may have high fees and expenses.
- **Benefits**: Annuities offer a guaranteed stream of income for life. Annuities can serve as a hedge against inflation.

It is important to note that these risks and benefits are not exhaustive, and investment options may vary in their level of risk and return.

It is important to consult with a financial advisor and do your own research before making any investment decisions for your retirement portfolio.

CHAPTER 5

MAXIMIZING YOUR SOCIAL SECURITY BENEFITS

I. Understanding Social Security Benefits

Social Security benefits are an important part of many retirees' income streams, providing a guaranteed source of income that can help support a fulfilling retirement. Understanding how Social Security works and how to maximize your benefits is essential for effective retirement planning.

Social Security benefits are based on your earnings history and the age at which you begin receiving benefits. The amount of your monthly benefit is determined by a complex formula that takes into account your highest 35 years of earnings, adjusted for inflation. The longer you wait to begin receiving benefits (up to age 70), the higher your monthly benefit will be.

To maximize your Social Security benefits, it's important to consider a range of factors, including your expected lifespan, financial needs, and overall retirement goals.

II. How to Maximize Your Social Security Benefits

Social Security benefits are an important source of income for many retirees, so it's important to maximize them as much as possible.

Here are some strategies to help you get the most out of your Social Security benefits:

1. **Delay claiming benefits:** You can begin claiming Social Security benefits as early as age 62, but if you delay claiming until your full retirement age (between 66 and 67 depending on your birth year), you can increase your benefits by up to 8% per year. If you delay claiming until age 70, your

benefits can increase by up to 32%.

2. **Coordinate spousal benefits:** If you're married, you may be eligible for spousal benefits based on your spouse's work history. You can claim these benefits as early as age 62, but delaying until your full retirement age can increase your benefits by up to 50% of your spouse's full retirement benefit amount.

3. **Consider survivor benefits:** If your spouse passes away, you may be eligible for survivor benefits based on their work history. These benefits can be up to 100% of your spouse's benefit amount. Delaying claiming survivor benefits until your full retirement age can maximize your benefits.

4. **Monitor your earnings history:** Your Social Security benefits are based on your average earnings over your working career, so it's important to make sure your earnings history is accurate. You can do this by reviewing your Social Security statement and reporting any errors or missing earnings to the Social Security Administration.

5. **Manage your taxes:** Social Security benefits may be subject to income tax, depending on your income level. To minimize the impact of taxes on your benefits, consider strategies such as delaying retirement account withdrawals or using tax-efficient investment vehicles.

6. **Consider Social Security as part of your overall retirement plan:** Social

Security benefits are just one piece of your overall retirement income picture. It's important to consider how Social Security fits into your overall retirement plan, and to develop a strategy that aligns with your goals and needs.

By following these strategies, you can maximize your Social Security benefits and ensure a more secure retirement income.

While Social Security benefits can be a valuable source of income in retirement, it's important to understand the complex rules and regulations governing these benefits. Working with a financial advisor or retirement planning professional can help you make the most of your Social Security benefits and achieve your retirement goals.

III. Key Factors That Affect Your Social Security Benefits

Social Security benefits are a crucial source of income for many retirees, but the amount you receive can vary greatly depending on several key factors.

Here are some of the main factors that affect your Social Security benefits:

1. **Your earnings history:** Your Social Security benefits are based on your average earnings over your working lifetime. The more you earned, the higher your benefits will be. Your earnings are adjusted for inflation and the highest 35 years of earnings are used to calculate your benefits.

2. **Your retirement age:** You can begin receiving Social Security benefits as early as age 62, but if you choose to begin receiving benefits before your full retirement age, your benefits will be permanently reduced. Your full retirement age depends on the year you were born, but it's generally between 66 and 67.

3. **Your spouse's earnings history:** If you're married, you may be eligible for spousal benefits based on your spouse's earnings history. The amount you can receive depends on your spouse's earnings and your age.

4. **Your work history:** If you worked for a government agency or a nonprofit organization that didn't withhold Social Security taxes,

your benefits may be reduced by the Windfall Elimination Provision or the Government Pension Offset.

5. **Your marital status:** If you're divorced, you may be eligible for benefits based on your ex-spouse's earnings history. You must have been married for at least 10 years and not currently married to be eligible.

6. **Your health status:** If you have a disability that prevents you from working, you may be eligible for Social Security Disability benefits. These benefits are based on your earnings history, and you must meet certain medical and work requirements to be eligible.

7. **Changes to the Social Security program:** The Social Security program is facing long-term

funding challenges, and changes to the program could affect the amount of benefits you receive in the future. It's important to stay informed about any changes to the program and adjust your retirement planning accordingly.

Understanding these key factors can help you make informed decisions about when to start receiving Social Security benefits and how to maximize your benefits over your lifetime.

IV. When to Claim Social Security Benefits

When to claim Social Security benefits is an important decision that can greatly affect your retirement income. You can start receiving Social Security retirement benefits as early as age 62, but the longer you wait to claim benefits, the larger your monthly benefit will be.

Here are some factors to consider when deciding when to claim Social Security benefits:

1. **Full Retirement Age (FRA):** Your FRA is the age at which you are eligible to receive 100% of your Social Security benefits. This age is based on your year of birth and ranges from 66 to 67. If you claim benefits before your FRA, your benefit will be permanently reduced. If you delay claiming benefits beyond your FRA, your benefit will increase by a certain percentage (depending on your year of birth) until you reach age 70.

2. **Health:** If you have health problems or a family history of shorter lifespans, you may want to consider claiming benefits early to maximize the amount you receive over your lifetime. On the other hand, if you are in good health and expect to live longer, delaying benefits can provide a larger monthly benefit and more total benefits over your lifetime.

3. **Current Financial Situation:** If you need the income now, claiming benefits early may be the best option. However, if you have other sources of income or savings that can cover your expenses, delaying benefits may provide a larger benefit in the long run.

4. **Spousal Benefits:** If you are married, divorced, or widowed, you may be eligible for spousal

benefits based on your spouse's work history. In some cases, delaying benefits can maximize the total amount of benefits you and your spouse receive over your lifetimes.

5. **Taxes:** Social Security benefits may be subject to federal income taxes if your income is above a certain threshold. Delaying benefits can help reduce your taxable income in the short term, which may help you avoid paying more in taxes.

In summary, deciding when to claim Social Security benefits requires careful consideration of your personal circumstances and financial goals. You may want to consult with a financial advisor or use online calculators to help you make an informed decision.

CHAPTER 6

MANAGING YOUR RETIREMENT INCOME

I. Retirement Income Strategies

Retirement income strategies involve managing your savings and investment accounts to provide income streams that cover your retirement expenses.

Here are some retirement income strategies to consider:

1. **Systematic Withdrawal:** This strategy involves withdrawing a

fixed amount of money from your retirement accounts at regular intervals, such as monthly or annually. The withdrawal amount is based on your projected retirement expenses and the expected rate of return on your investments.

2. **Immediate Annuities:** An immediate annuity provides guaranteed income for life in exchange for a lump sum payment. With an immediate annuity, you receive a fixed amount of income each month, regardless of market conditions.

3. **Deferred Annuities:** Deferred annuities provide a stream of income in the future, usually starting at retirement age. The annuity is funded by regular contributions or a lump sum

payment, and the income is based on the account balance and the annuity contract terms.

4. **Bond Laddering:** This strategy involves investing in a series of bonds with different maturities to provide a steady stream of income. As each bond matures, the principal is reinvested in a new bond with a longer maturity.

5. **Dividend Income:** Dividend-paying stocks and mutual funds can provide a reliable source of income in retirement. The income is generated by the dividend payments, which are typically paid quarterly.

6. **Rental Income:** Real estate investments can provide rental income to supplement your retirement income. Rental income

can be generated from residential or commercial properties.

7. **Part-Time Work:** If you are able and willing to work in retirement, part-time work can provide additional income to supplement your retirement savings.

It's important to remember that each retirement income strategy has its own set of advantages and disadvantages. Consider your personal financial situation, risk tolerance, and retirement goals when choosing a strategy that works best for you. A financial advisor can also provide guidance on developing a retirement income strategy that meets your needs.

II. How to Create a Sustainable Retirement Income Plan

Creating a sustainable retirement income plan is essential for ensuring that you have enough money to last throughout your retirement.

Here are some steps you can take to create a sustainable retirement income plan:

1. **Determine your retirement income needs:** The first step in creating a sustainable retirement income plan is to determine how much income you will need in retirement. Consider your lifestyle goals, healthcare expenses, housing costs, and other expenses.

2. **Estimate your retirement income sources:** Next, estimate the sources of retirement income you will have, such as Social Security, pensions, retirement accounts, and other investments. Calculate the total amount of income you can expect to receive from these sources.

3. **Develop a withdrawal strategy:** Once you have determined your retirement income needs and sources, develop a withdrawal strategy. This strategy should consider the tax implications of withdrawing from different accounts, as well as the timing of withdrawals.

4. **Consider annuities:** Annuities can provide a guaranteed stream of income in retirement. Consider

incorporating an annuity into your retirement income plan.

5. **Manage your investment portfolio:** Your investment portfolio can play a significant role in your retirement income plan. Consider a balanced portfolio that includes stocks, bonds, and other investments. Also, consider the impact of inflation on your portfolio.

6. **Monitor and adjust your plan:** As you move through retirement, it's essential to monitor and adjust your plan as needed. Changes in your lifestyle goals, health, and other factors may require adjustments to your retirement income plan.

Creating a sustainable retirement income plan can be complex. Consider working with a financial advisor to develop a plan that meets your specific needs and goals.

With a sound retirement income plan, you can have peace of mind knowing that you have the resources you need to enjoy your retirement.

III. Tax Implications of Different Retirement Income Sources

Retirement income from different sources can have different tax implications, and understanding these implications can help retirees make informed decisions about their retirement income plan.

Here are some key tax considerations for common retirement income sources:

1. **Social Security Benefits:** Social Security benefits can be subject to federal income tax depending on your income level. The IRS uses a formula called the "combined income" formula to determine whether your benefits will be taxed. Combined income is calculated as your adjusted gross income (AGI) plus any non-taxable interest plus half of your Social Security benefits. If your combined income is above a certain threshold, up to 85% of your Social Security benefits may be subject to federal income tax.

2. **Retirement Account Distributions:** Distributions from

traditional IRAs, 401(k)s, and other retirement accounts are generally taxable as ordinary income. Roth IRA distributions, on the other hand, are generally tax-free as long as certain requirements are met.

3. **Annuity Payments:** Annuity payments may be taxable as ordinary income or partially tax-free, depending on the type of annuity and the source of the premiums. If you paid premiums with after-tax dollars, a portion of the annuity payment may be tax-free.

4. **Investment Income:** Investment income, such as interest, dividends, and capital gains, can be subject to federal income tax as well as state and local taxes. Tax rates on investment income can

vary depending on your income level, the type of investment, and how long you held the investment.

5. **Rental Income:** Rental income from real estate can be subject to federal income tax, state and local taxes, and self-employment taxes if you actively manage the property. However, there are deductions and credits available for rental property owners that can help reduce their tax liability.

It's important to consider the tax implications of different retirement income sources when developing a retirement income plan. A financial advisor or tax professional can help you navigate the complex tax rules and develop a tax-efficient retirement income strategy.

IV. Strategies for Managing Your Retirement Income

Retirement is a time when most people rely heavily on their retirement savings and investment income to maintain their lifestyle. Hence, it's important to have a strategy for managing retirement income.

Here are some strategies to consider:

1. **Develop a withdrawal strategy:** A withdrawal strategy is an essential part of managing your retirement income. One approach is the "4% rule," which suggests withdrawing 4% of your retirement savings each year. However, this approach may not

work for everyone, and it's essential to consider other factors, such as taxes, investment returns, and inflation.

2. **Consider delaying Social Security benefits:** Delaying your Social Security benefits can increase your monthly payments by up to 8% per year. This strategy may be useful if you don't need the income immediately and want to maximize your payments over time.

3. **Diversify your retirement income sources:** Relying on a single source of retirement income can be risky. Diversifying your income sources, such as Social Security, pension, investment income, and part-time work, can help ensure a steady stream of income during retirement.

4. **Use tax-efficient withdrawal strategies:** Withdrawals from retirement accounts, such as 401(k)s and traditional IRAs, are typically taxed at ordinary income tax rates. However, using tax-efficient withdrawal strategies, such as withdrawing from tax-free or tax-deferred accounts first, can help reduce your tax liability.

5. **Consider annuities:** An annuity is a financial product that provides a guaranteed income stream for a specific period or for life. Annuities can be a valuable addition to your retirement income strategy, but it's important to consider the costs and potential drawbacks before purchasing one.

6. **Review and adjust your retirement income plan regularly:** It's essential to review your retirement income plan regularly to ensure that it's still meeting your needs and goals. As your circumstances change, you may need to adjust your plan to ensure a sustainable retirement income.

In summary, managing retirement income requires careful planning and consideration of various factors, including tax implications, diversification, and withdrawal strategies. By developing a sound retirement income plan and regularly reviewing and adjusting it, you can help ensure a sustainable and fulfilling retirement.

CHAPTER 7

ESTATE PLANNING IN RETIREMENT

I. Importance of Estate Planning

Estate planning is a crucial aspect of retirement planning that often gets overlooked. It involves making decisions about how your assets will be distributed after your death, as well as addressing other important issues such as healthcare decisions and guardianship for minor children.

One of the primary benefits of estate planning is that it allows you to maintain control over how your assets are distributed after your death. This is particularly important if you have specific wishes or concerns regarding who should inherit your assets or if you want to minimize estate taxes.

Another key aspect of estate planning is ensuring that your healthcare and end-of-life decisions are respected. This includes appointing a trusted person to make medical decisions on your behalf if you become incapacitated, as well as making your wishes regarding life-sustaining treatment and other medical interventions clear.

Estate planning can also help you protect your assets from creditors and legal challenges. By creating a comprehensive estate plan, you can ensure that your assets are distributed according to your wishes and that your loved ones are protected from any potential legal disputes.

Overall, estate planning is an important part of retirement planning that should not be overlooked. By taking the time to create a comprehensive estate plan, you can ensure that your wishes are respected, your assets are protected, and your loved ones are taken care of after your death.

II. Key Elements of Estate Planning

Estate planning involves making arrangements for the distribution of your assets after you pass away. It is a critical part of retirement planning as it ensures that your assets are passed down according to your wishes, and it can also help minimize the tax burden on your beneficiaries.

The following are key elements of estate planning that retirees should consider:

1. Will

A will is a legal document that outlines how you want your assets distributed after you die. It can also name an executor to manage your estate and provide for the care of any dependents.

2. Trusts

Trusts are legal arrangements in which you transfer your assets to a trustee who manages them on behalf of your beneficiaries. Trusts can be used to minimize estate taxes and provide for the long-term care of beneficiaries.

3. Power of Attorney

A power of attorney is a legal document that grants another person the authority to make financial and legal decisions on your behalf if you become incapacitated.

4. Advance Directives

Advance directives are legal documents that outline your wishes for medical care if you are unable to make decisions for yourself. These documents include a living will, which outlines your preferences for life-sustaining treatments, and a healthcare power of attorney, which designates a person to make medical decisions on your behalf.

5. Beneficiary Designations

Retirement accounts and life insurance policies require you to name beneficiaries who will receive the assets upon your death. It is important to review and update these designations regularly to ensure they align with your current wishes.

6. Tax Planning

Estate planning can help minimize the tax burden on your beneficiaries by utilizing strategies such as gifting, charitable donations, and establishing trusts.

7. Business Succession Planning: If you own a business, it is important to consider how it will be managed and passed down after you retire or pass away. Business succession planning can

help ensure a smooth transition and preserve the value of your business for your heirs.

In conclusion, estate planning is a critical part of retirement planning that involves making arrangements for the distribution of your assets after you pass away. Key elements of estate planning include a will, trusts, power of attorney, advance directives, beneficiary designations, tax planning, and business succession planning. It is important to work with a qualified attorney or financial advisor to develop an estate plan that aligns with your wishes and financial goals.

III. How to Create a Comprehensive Estate Plan

Creating a comprehensive estate plan is an important step in preparing for your retirement and ensuring your assets are distributed according to your wishes.

When creating your estate plan, it is important to work with an experienced estate planning attorney to ensure that your wishes are properly documented and that your estate plan complies with all applicable laws and regulations.

You should also review and update your estate plan regularly to ensure that it reflects your current wishes and circumstances.

IV. Common Estate Planning Mistakes to Avoid

Estate planning is an important part of retirement planning that ensures your assets are distributed according to your wishes after you pass away.

However, many people make common estate planning mistakes that can result in unintended consequences, legal disputes, and increased costs.

In this section, we will discuss some of the most common estate planning mistakes to avoid.

1. Not having an estate plan

The most common estate planning mistake is not having an estate plan at all. According to a survey conducted by Caring.com, only 32% of American adults have a will or estate planning documents in place. This means that the majority of people risk having their assets distributed according to state law, which may not reflect their wishes.

2. **Failing to update estate planning documents**

Another common estate planning mistake is failing to update estate planning documents. Your circumstances, assets, and beneficiaries may change over time, and it's important to ensure that your estate plan reflects these changes. Failing to update your estate plan can lead to unintended consequences and legal disputes.

3. **Not considering tax implications**

Estate planning involves more than just distributing your assets to your beneficiaries. It also involves minimizing tax liabilities. Failing to consider tax implications can result in your beneficiaries receiving less than you intended or even losing a portion of their inheritance to taxes.

4. Neglecting to name beneficiaries

Naming beneficiaries is an important part of estate planning. Neglecting to name beneficiaries or failing to update beneficiary designations can result in unintended consequences, such as the wrong person receiving assets or assets going to the estate instead of to beneficiaries.

5. Not considering the needs of beneficiaries

It's important to consider the needs of your beneficiaries when creating your estate plan. For example, if you have a beneficiary with special needs, you may need to create a special needs trust to ensure that their inheritance doesn't disqualify them from receiving government benefits.

6. Failing to plan for incapacity

Estate planning is not just about what happens after you pass away. It's also about planning for incapacity. Failing to plan for incapacity can result in your loved ones being unable to make decisions on your behalf if you become incapacitated.

7. Not seeking professional advice

Estate planning is complex, and it's important to seek professional advice from an estate planning attorney or financial advisor. Failing to seek professional advice can result in mistakes and unintended consequences.

In conclusion, estate planning is an important part of retirement planning, and it's important to avoid common estate planning mistakes.

By creating an estate plan, updating it regularly, considering tax implications, naming beneficiaries, planning for the needs of beneficiaries, planning for incapacity, and seeking professional advice, you can ensure that your assets are distributed according to your wishes and your loved ones are taken care of after you pass away.

CHAPTER 8

CONCLUSION

I. Recap of Key Points

The Retirement Planning Guide aims to provide a comprehensive overview of retirement planning, from understanding the importance of retirement planning to developing a retirement plan and managing retirement income.

Throughout the guide, we discussed the following key points:

1. Retirement planning is crucial to ensure a fulfilling life in your senior years.

2. Common retirement planning mistakes include not starting early enough, not considering healthcare costs, and underestimating expenses.

3. It's essential to assess your retirement needs, including estimating retirement expenses, evaluating sources of retirement income, and calculating a retirement savings goal.

4. Retirement plans can include employer-sponsored plans, individual retirement accounts (IRAs), and annuities, each with their own benefits and drawbacks.

5. Investment strategies for retirement should be based on

your risk tolerance and long-term financial goals.

6. Maximizing Social Security benefits involves understanding the key factors that affect your benefits, when to claim benefits, and how to optimize your benefits.

7. Retirement income strategies should focus on creating a sustainable retirement income plan that considers tax implications and potential inflation.

8. Estate planning is important to ensure that your assets are distributed according to your wishes after you pass away.

9. Common estate planning mistakes include not updating your plan regularly and failing to communicate your wishes to your family members.

By following the guidelines and strategies presented in this guide, you can be better equipped to design a fulfilling life in your senior years. Remember, it's never too early or too late to start planning for your retirement.

II. Next Steps in Your Retirement Planning Journey

Congratulations on completing the retirement planning guide and taking the first step towards securing a fulfilling life in your senior years. As you embark on your retirement planning journey, here are some next steps to consider:

1. **Take action:** Implement the strategies and recommendations

outlined in this guide. Start by assessing your retirement needs, creating a retirement plan, and investing for retirement.

2. **Consult a financial advisor:** A financial advisor can help you navigate complex financial decisions, provide personalized advice, and help you stay on track towards achieving your retirement goals.

3. **Review your plan regularly:** As your circumstances change, such as a change in job or family status, you may need to adjust your retirement plan accordingly. It is important to review your plan regularly to ensure that you are on track towards your retirement goals.

4. **Stay informed:** Keep yourself updated on retirement planning

news and trends. Stay informed on changes to retirement laws and regulations, and be aware of new investment opportunities that may help you reach your goals.

Remember, retirement planning is a journey, and it is never too late or too early to start. By taking action today and following the steps outlined in this guide, you can achieve a fulfilling retirement and live the life you have always dreamed of.

III. Resources for Further Learning and Support.

Here are some resources that you may find helpful in your retirement planning journey:

1. **Social Security Administration**: The official website of the Social Security Administration provides a wealth of information on retirement benefits, disability benefits, survivor benefits, and more. You can also use the website to estimate your future Social Security benefits.

2. **AARP**: The AARP (formerly known as the American Association of Retired Persons) is a nonprofit organization that provides a wide range of resources and support for people over the age of 50. Their website offers articles, tools, and calculators to help you with retirement planning, as well as information on healthcare, travel, and other topics of interest to seniors.

3. **National Institute on Retirement Security:** The National Institute on Retirement Security is a nonprofit organization that conducts research and provides education on retirement security issues. Their website offers reports, white papers, and other resources on retirement planning, as well as a blog that covers the latest news and trends in retirement security.

4. **Financial Planning Association**: The Financial Planning Association is a professional organization for financial planners. Their website includes a directory of certified financial planners, as well as resources on retirement planning, investing, and other financial topics.

ACKNOWLEDGMENTS

I would like to express my heartfelt gratitude to all the experts and professionals who contributed their knowledge and expertise to this guidebook. I am deeply grateful to them for sharing their insights and experiences on retirement planning, and for their commitment to helping others achieve their retirement goals.

I would also like to thank my editorial team for their tireless efforts in editing and refining the content of this guidebook. Their attention to detail and dedication to producing a high-quality resource have been invaluable.

Finally, I extend my thanks to my readers for choosing "The Complete Retirement Planning Handbook 2023" as a guide in their retirement planning journey. I hope that this guidebook helps you to achieve a stress-free and fulfilling retirement.

www.ingramcontent.com/pod-product-compliance
Lightning Source LLC
Chambersburg PA
CBHW070557220526
45467CB00003B/1227